Diary of a Lunatic/Three D

by Leo Tolsto,,

Translated by Constance Garnett

Translated by Nathan Haskell Dole

Diary of a Lunatic

by Leo Tolstoy,

Translated by Constance Garnett

This morning I underwent a medical examination in the government council room. The opinions of the doctors were divided. They argued among themselves and came at last to the conclusion that I was not mad. But this was due to the fact that I tried hard during the examination not to give myself away. I was afraid of being sent to the lunatic asylum, where I would not be able to go on with the mad undertaking I have on my hands. They pronounced me subject to fits of excitement, and something else, too, but nevertheless of sound mind. The doctor prescribed a certain treatment, and assured me that by following his directions my trouble would completely disappear. Imagine, all that torments me disappearing completely! Oh, there is nothing I would not give to be free from my trouble. The suffering is too great!

I am going to tell explicitly how I came to undergo that examination; how I went mad, and how my madness was revealed to the outside world.

Up to the age of thirty-five I lived like the rest of the world, and nobody had noticed any peculiarities in me. Only in my early childhood, before I was ten, I had occasionally been in a mental state similar to the present one, and then only at intervals, whereas now I am continually conscious of it.

I remember going to bed one evening, when I was a child of five or six. Nurse Euprasia, a tall, lean woman in a brown dress, with a double chin, was undressing me, and was just lifting me up to put me into bed.

"I will get into bed myself," I said, preparing to step over the net at the bedside.

"Lie down, Fedinka. You see, Mitinka is already lying quite still," she said, pointing with her head to my brother in his bed.

I jumped into my bed still holding nurse's hand in mine. Then I let it go, stretched my legs under the blanket and wrapped myself up. I felt so nice and warm! I grew silent all of a sudden and began thinking: "I love nurse, nurse loves me and Mitinka, I love Mitinka too, and he loves me and nurse. And nurse loves Taras; I love Taras too, and so does Mitinka. And Taras loves me and nurse. And mother loves me and nurse, nurse loves mother and me and father; everybody loves everybody, and everybody is happy."

Suddenly the housekeeper rushed in and began to shout in an angry voice something about a sugar basin she could not find. Nurse got cross and said she did not take it. I felt frightened; it was all so strange. A cold horror came over me, and I hid myself under the blanket. But I felt no better in the darkness under the blanket. I thought of a boy who had got a thrashing one day in my presence - of his screams, and of the cruel face of Foka when he was beating the boy.

"Then you won't do it any more; you won't!" he repeated and went on beating.

"I won't," said the boy; and Foka kept on repeating over and over, "You won't, you won't!" and did not cease to strike the boy.

That was when my madness came over me for the first time. I burst into sobs, and they could not quiet me for a long while. The tears and despair of that day were the first signs of my present trouble.

I well remember the second time my madness seized me. It was when aunt was telling us about Christ. She told His story and got up to leave the room. But we held her back: "Tell us more about Jesus Christ!" we said.

"I must go," she replied.

"No, tell us more, please!" Mitinka insisted, and she repeated all she had said before. She told us how they crucified Him, how they beat and martyred Him, and how He went on praying and did not blame them.

"Auntie, why did they torture Him?"

"They were wicked."

"But wasn't he God?"

"Be still - it is nine o'clock, don't you hear the clock striking?"

"Why did they beat Him? He had forgiven them. Then why did they hit Him? Did it hurt Him? Auntie, did it hurt?"

"Be quiet, I say. I am going to the dining-room to have tea now."

"But perhaps it never happened, perhaps He was not beaten by them?"

"I am going."

"No, Auntie, don't go!..." And again my madness took possession of me. I sobbed and sobbed, and began knocking my head against the wall.

Such had been the fits of my madness in my childhood. But after I was fourteen, from the time the instincts of sex awoke and I began to give way to vice, my madness seemed to have passed, and I was a boy like other boys. Just as happens with all of us who are brought up on rich, over-abundant food, and are spoiled and made effeminate, because we never do any physical work, and are surrounded by all possible temptations, which excite our sensual nature when in the company of other children similarly spoiled, so I had been taught vice by other boys of my age and I indulged in it. As time passed other vices came to take the place of the first. I began to know women, and so I went on living, up to the time I was thirty-five, looking out for all kinds of pleasures and enjoying them. I had a perfectly sound mind then, and never a sign of madness. Those twenty years of my normal life passed without leaving any special record on my memory, and now it is only with a great effort of mind and with utter disgust, that I can concentrate my thoughts upon that time.

Like all the boys of my set, who were of sound mind, I entered school, passed on to the university and went through a course of law studies. Then I entered the State service for a short time, married, and settled down in the country, educating - if our way of bringing up children can be called educating - my children, looking after the land, and filling the post of a Justice of the Peace.

It was when I had been married ten years that one of those attacks of madness I suffered from in my childhood made its appearance again. My wife and I had saved up money from her inheritance and from some Government bonds of mine which I had sold, and we decided that with that money we would buy another estate. I was naturally keen to increase our fortune, and to do it in the shrewdest way, better than any one else would manage it. I went about inquiring what estates were to be sold, and used to read all the advertisements in the papers. What I wanted was to buy an estate, the produce or timber of which would cover the cost of purchase, and then I would have the estate practically for nothing. I was looking out for a fool who did not understand business, and there came a day when I thought I had found one. An estate with large forests attached to it was to be sold in the Pensa Government. To judge by the information I had received the proprietor of that estate was exactly the imbecile I wanted, and I might expect the forests to cover the price asked for the whole estate. I got my things ready and was soon on my way to the estate I wished to inspect.

We had first to go by train (I had taken my man-servant with me), then by coach, with relays of horses at the various stations. The journey was very pleasant, and my servant, a good-natured youth, liked it as much as I did. We enjoyed the new surroundings and the new people, and having now only about two hundred miles more to drive, we decided to go on without stopping, except to change horses at the stations. Night came on and we were still driving. I had been dozing, but presently I awoke, seized with a sudden fear. As often happens in such a case, I was so excited that I was thoroughly awake and it seemed as if sleep were gone for ever. "Why am I driving? Where am I going?" I suddenly asked myself. It was not that I disliked the idea of buying an estate at a bargain, but it seemed at that moment so senseless to journey to such a far away place, and I had a feeling as if I were going to die there, away from home. I was overcome with terror.

My servant Sergius awoke, and I took advantage of the fact to talk to him. I began to remark upon the scenery around us; he had also a good deal to say, of the people at home, of the pleasure of the journey, and it seemed strange to me that he could talk so gaily. He appeared so pleased with everything and in such good spirits, whereas I was annoyed with it all. Still, I felt more at ease when I was talking with him. Along with my feelings of restlessness and my secret horror, however, I was fatigued as well, and longed to break the journey somewhere. It seemed to me my uneasiness would cease if I could only enter a room, have tea, and, what I desired most of all, sleep.

We were approaching the town Arzamas.

"Don't you think we had better stop here and have a rest?"

"Why not? It's an excellent idea."

"How far are we from the town?" I asked the driver.

"Another seven miles."

The driver was a quiet, silent man. He was driving rather slowly and wearily.

We drove on. I was silent, but I felt better, looking forward to a rest and hoping to feel the better for it. We drove on and on in the darkness, and the seven miles seemed to have no end. At last we reached the town. It was sound asleep at that early hour. First came the small houses, piercing the darkness, and as we passed them, the noise of our jingling bells and the trotting of our horses sounded louder. In a few places the houses were large and white, but I did not feel less dejected for seeing them. I was waiting for the station, and the samovar, and longed to lie down and rest.

At last we approached a house with pillars in front of it. The house was white, but it seemed to me very melancholy. I felt even frightened at its aspect and stepped slowly out of the carriage. Sergius was busying himself with our luggage, taking what we needed for the night, running about and stepping heavily on the doorsteps. The sound of his brisk tread increased my weariness. I walked in and came into a small passage. A man received us; he had a large spot on his cheek and that spot filled me with horror. He asked us into a room which was just an ordinary room. My uneasiness was growing.

"Could we have a room to rest in?" I asked.

"Oh, yes, I have a very nice bedroom at your disposal. A square room, newly whitewashed."

The fact of the little room being square was - I remember it so well - most painful to me. It had one window with a red curtain, a table of birchwood and a sofa with a curved back and arms. Sergius boiled the water in the samovar and made the tea. I put a pillow on the sofa in the meantime and lay down. I was not asleep; I heard Sergius busy with the samovar and urging me to have tea. I was afraid to get up from the sofa, afraid of driving away sleep; and just to be sitting in that room seemed awful. I did not get up, but fell into a sort of doze. When I started up out of it, nobody was in the room and it was quite dark. I woke up with the very same sensation I had the first time and knew sleep was gone. "Why am I here? Where am I going? Just as I am I must be for ever. Neither the Pensa nor any other estate will add to or take anything away from me. As for me, I am unbearably weary of myself. I want to go to sleep, to forget - and I cannot, I cannot get rid of self."

I went out into the passage. Sergius was sleeping there on a narrow bench, his hand hanging down beside it. He was sleeping soundly, and the man with the spot on his cheek was also asleep. I thought, by going out of the room, to get away from what was tormenting me. But it followed me and made everything seem dark and dreary. My feeling of horror, instead of leaving me, was increasing.

"What nonsense!" I said to myself. "Why am I so dejected? What am I afraid of?" "You are afraid of me" - I heard the voice of Death - "I am here."

I shuddered. Yes, - Death! Death will come, it will come and it ought not to come. Even in facing actual death I would certainly not feel anything of what I felt now. Then it would be simply fear, whereas now it was more than that. I was actually seeing, feeling the approach of death, and along with it I felt that death ought not to exist.

My entire being was conscious of the necessity of the right to live, and at the same time of the inevitability of dying. This inner conflict was causing me unbearable pain. I tried to shake off the horror; I found a half-burnt candle in a brass candlestick and lighted it. The candle with its red flame burnt down until it was not much taller than the low candlestick. The same thing seemed to be repeated over and over: nothing lasts, life is not, all is death - but death ought not to exist. I tried to turn my thoughts to what had interested me before, to the estate I was to buy and to my wife. Far from being a relief, these seemed nothing to me now. To feel my life doomed to be taken from me was a terror shutting out any other thought. "I must try to sleep," I decided. I went to bed, but the next instant I jumped up, seized with horror. A sickness overcame me, a spiritual sickness not unlike the physical uneasiness preceding actual illness - but in the spirit, not in the body. A terrible fear similar to the fear of death, when mingled with the recollections of my past life, developed into a horror as if life were departing. Life and death were flowing into one another. An unknown power was trying to tear my soul into pieces, but could not bend it. Once more I went out into the passage to look at the two men asleep; once more I tried to go to sleep. The horror was always the same - now red, now white and square. Something was tearing within but could not be torn apart. A torturing sensation! An arid hatred deprived me of every spark of kindly feeling. Just a dull and steady hatred against myself and against that which had created me. What did create me? God? We say God.... "What if I tried to pray?" I suddenly thought. I had not said a prayer for more than twenty years and I had no religious sentiment, although just for formality's sake I fasted and partook of the communion every year. I began saying prayers; "God, forgive me," "Our Father," "Our Lady," I was composing new prayers, crossing myself, bowing to the earth, looking around me all the while for fear I might be discovered in my devotional attitude. The prayers seemed to divert my thoughts from the previous terror, but it was more the fear of being seen by somebody that did it. I went to bed again. but the moment I shut my eyes the very same feeling of terror made me jump up. I could not stand it any longer. I called the hotel servant, roused Sergius from his sleep, ordered him to harness the horses to the carriage and we were soon driving on once more. The open air and the drive made me feel much better. But I realised that something new had come into my soul, and had poisoned the life I had lived up to that hour.

We reached our destination in the evening. The whole day long I remained struggling with despair, and finally conquered it; but a horror remained in the depth of my soul. It was as if a misfortune had happened to me, and although I was able to forget it for a while, it remained at the bottom of my soul, and I was entirely dominated by it.

The manager of the estate, an old man, received us in a very friendly manner, though not exactly with great joy; he was sorry that the estate was to be sold. The clean little rooms with upholstered furniture, a new, shining samovar on the tea-table, nice large cups, honey served with the tea, - everything was pleasant to see. I began questioning him about the estate without any interest, as if I were repeating a lesson learned long ago and nearly forgotten. It was so uninteresting. But that night I was able to go to sleep without feeling miserable. I thought this was due to having said my

prayers again before going to bed.

After that incident I resumed my ordinary life; but the apprehension that this horror would again come upon me was continual. I had to live my usual life without any respite, not giving way to my thoughts, just like a schoolboy who repeats by habit and without thinking the lesson learned by heart. That was the only way to avoid being seized again by the horror and the despair I had experienced in Arzamas.

I had returned home safe from my journey; I had not bought the estate - I had not enough money. My life at home seemed to be just as it had always been, save for my having taken to saying prayers and to going to church. But now, when I recollect that time, I see that I only imagined my life to be the same as before. The fact was I merely continued what I had previously started, and was running with the same speed on rails already laid; but I did not undertake anything new.

Even in those things which I had already taken in hand my interest had diminished. I was tired of everything, and was growing very religious. My wife noticed this, and was often vexed with me for it. No new fit of distress occurred while I was at home. But one day I had to go unexpectedly to Moscow, where a lawsuit was pending. In the train I entered into conversation with a land-owner from Kharkov. We were talking about the management of estates, about bank business, about the hotels in Moscow, and the theatres. We both decided to stop at the "Moscow Court," in the Miasnizkaia Street, and go that evening to the opera, to Faust. When we arrived I was shown into a small room, the heavy smell of the passage being still in my nostrils. the porter brought in my portmanteau, and the amid lighted the candle, the flame of which burned up brightly and then flickered, as it usually does. In the room next to mine I heard somebody coughing, probably an old man. The maid went out, and

adding each time, "Reveal Thy existence to me!" I became quiet, waiting for an answer. But no answer came, as if there were nothing to answer. I was alone, alone with myself and was answering my own questions in place of him who would not answer. "What am I created for?" "To live in a future life," I answered. "Then why this uncertainty and torment? I cannot believe in future life. I did believe when I asked, but not with my whole soul. Now I cannot, I cannot! If Thou didst exist, Thou wouldst reveal it to me, to all men. But Thou dost not exist, and there is nothing true but distress." But I cannot accept that! I rebelled against it; I implored Him to reveal His existence to me. I did all that everybody does, but He did not reveal Himself to me. "Ask and it shall be given unto you," I remembered, and began to entreat; in doing so I felt no real comfort, but just surcease of despair. Perhaps it was not entreaty on my part, but only denial of Him. You retreat a step from Him, and He goes from you a mile. I did not believe in Him, and yet here I was entreating Him. But He did not reveal Himself. I was balancing my accounts with Him, and was blaming Him. I simply did not believe.

The next day I used all my endeavors to get through with my affairs somehow during the day, in order to be saved from another night in the hotel room. Although I had not finished everything, I left for home in the evening.

That night at Moscow brought a still greater change into my life, which had been changing ever since the night at Arzamas. I was now paying less attention to my affairs, and grew more and more indifferent to everything around me. my health was also getting bad. My wife urged me to consult a doctor. To her my continual talk about God and religion was a sign of ill-health, whereas I knew I was ill and weak, because of the unsolved questions of religion and of God.

prayers again before going to bed.

After that incident I resumed my ordinary life; but the apprehension that this horror would again come upon me was continual. I had to live my usual life without any respite, not giving way to my thoughts, just like a schoolboy who repeats by habit and without thinking the lesson learned by heart. That was the only way to avoid being seized again by the horror and the despair I had experienced in Arzamas.

I had returned home safe from my journey; I had not bought the estate - I had not enough money. My life at home seemed to be just as it had always been, save for my having taken to saying prayers and to going to church. But now, when I recollect that time, I see that I only imagined my life to be the same as before. The fact was I merely continued what I had previously started, and was running with the same speed on rails already laid; but I did not undertake anything new.

Even in those things which I had already taken in hand my interest had diminished. I was tired of everything, and was growing very religious. My wife noticed this, and was often vexed with me for it. No new fit of distress occurred while I was at home. But one day I had to go unexpectedly to Moscow, where a lawsuit was pending. In the train I entered into conversation with a land-owner from Kharkov. We were talking about the management of estates, about bank business, about the hotels in Moscow, and the theatres. We both decided to stop at the "Moscow Court," in the Miasnizkaia Street, and go that evening to the opera, to Faust. When we arrived I was shown into a small room, the heavy smell of the passage being still in my nostrils. the porter brought in my portmanteau, and the amid lighted the candle, the flame of which burned up brightly and then flickered, as it usually does. In the room next to mine I heard somebody coughing, probably an old man. The maid went out, and

adding each time, "Reveal Thy existence to me!" I became quiet, waiting for an answer. But no answer came, as if there were nothing to answer. I was alone, alone with myself and was answering my own questions in place of him who would not answer. "What am I created for?" "To live in a future life," I answered. "Then why this uncertainty and torment? I cannot believe in future life. I did believe when I asked, but not with my whole soul. Now I cannot, I cannot! If Thou didst exist, Thou wouldst reveal it to me, to all men. But Thou dost not exist, and there is nothing true but distress." But I cannot accept that! I rebelled against it; I implored Him to reveal His existence to me. I did all that everybody does, but He did not reveal Himself to me. "Ask and it shall be given unto you," I remembered, and began to entreat; in doing so I felt no real comfort, but just surcease of despair. Perhaps it was not entreaty on my part, but only denial of Him. You retreat a step from Him, and He goes from you a mile. I did not believe in Him, and yet here I was entreating Him. But He did not reveal Himself. I was balancing my accounts with Him, and was blaming Him. I simply did not believe.

The next day I used all my endeavors to get through with my affairs somehow during the day, in order to be saved from another night in the hotel room. Although I had not finished everything, I left for home in the evening.

That night at Moscow brought a still greater change into my life, which had been changing ever since the night at Arzamas. I was now paying less attention to my affairs, and grew more and more indifferent to everything around me. my health was also getting bad. My wife urged me to consult a doctor. To her my continual talk about God and religion was a sign of ill-health, whereas I knew I was ill and weak, because of the unsolved questions of religion and of God.

prayers again before going to bed.

After that incident I resumed my ordinary life; but the apprehension that this horror would again come upon me was continual. I had to live my usual life without any respite, not giving way to my thoughts, just like a schoolboy who repeats by habit and without thinking the lesson learned by heart. That was the only way to avoid being seized again by the horror and the despair I had experienced in Arzamas.

I had returned home safe from my journey; I had not bought the estate - I had not enough money. My life at home seemed to be just as it had always been, save for my having taken to saying prayers and to going to church. But now, when I recollect that time, I see that I only imagined my life to be the same as before. The fact was I merely continued what I had previously started, and was running with the same speed on rails already laid; but I did not undertake anything new.

Even in those things which I had already taken in hand my interest had diminished. I was tired of everything, and was growing very religious. My wife noticed this, and was often vexed with me for it. No new fit of distress occurred while I was at home. But one day I had to go unexpectedly to Moscow, where a lawsuit was pending. In the train I entered into conversation with a land-owner from Kharkov. We were talking about the management of estates, about bank business, about the hotels in Moscow, and the theatres. We both decided to stop at the "Moscow Court," in the Miasnizkaia Street, and go that evening to the opera, to Faust. When we arrived I was shown into a small room, the heavy smell of the passage being still in my nostrils. the porter brought in my portmanteau, and the amid lighted the candle, the flame of which burned up brightly and then flickered, as it usually does. In the room next to mine I heard somebody coughing, probably an old man. The maid went out, and

the porter asked whether I wished him to open my bag. In the meanwhile the candle flame had flared up, throwing its light on the blue wallpaper with yellow stripes, on the partition, on the shabby table, on the small sofa in the front of it, on the mirror hanging on the wall, and on the window. I saw what the small room was like, and suddenly felt the horror of the Arzamas night awakening within me.

"My God! Must I stay here for the night? How can I?" I thought. "Will you kindly unfasten my bag?" I said to the porter, to keep him longer in the room. "And now I'll dress quickly and go to the theatre," I said to myself.

When the bag had been untied I said to the porter, "Please tell the gentleman in Number 8 - the one who came with me - that I shall be ready presently, and ask him to wait for me."

The porter left, and I began to dress in haste, afraid to look at the walls. "But what nonsense!" I said to myself. "Why am I frightened like a child? I am not afraid of ghosts -" Ghosts! - to be afraid of ghosts is nothing to what I was afraid of! "But what is it? Absolutely nothing. I am only afraid of myself....Nonsense!"

I slipped into a cold, rough, starched shirt, stuck in the studs, put on evening dress and new boots, and went to call for the Kharkov landowner, who was ready. We started for the opera house. He stopped on the way to have his hair curled, while I went to a French hairdresser to have mine cut, where I talked a little to the Frenchwoman in the shop and bought a pair of gloves. Everything seemed all right. I had completely forgotten the oblong room in the hotel, and the walls.

I enjoyed the Faust performance very much, and when it was over my companion proposed that we should have supper. This was contrary to my habits; but just at that moment I remembered the walls in my room, and accepted.

We returned home after one. I had two glasses of wine - an unusual thing for me - in spite of which I was feeling quite at ease.

But the moment we entered the passage with the lowered lamp lighting it, the moment I was surrounded by the peculiar smell of the hotel. I felt a cold shudder of horror running down my back. But there was nothing to be done. I shook hands with my new friend, and stepped into my room.

I had a frightful night - much worse than the night at Arzamas; and it was not until dawn, when the old man in the next room was coughing again, that I fell asleep - and then not in my bed, but, after getting in and out of it many times, on the sofa.

I suffered the whole night unbearably. Once more my soul and my body were tearing themselves apart within me. the same thoughts came again: "I am living, I have lived up till now, I have the right to live; but all around me is death and destruction. Then why live? Why not die? Why not kill myself immediately? No; I could not. I am afraid. Is it better to wait for death to come when it will? No, that is even worse; and I am also afraid of that. Then, I must live. But what for? In order to die?" I could not get out of that circle. I took a book, and began reading. For a moment it made me forget my thoughts. But then the same questions and the same horror came again. I got into bed, lay down, and shut my eyes. That made the horror worse. God had created things as they are. But why? They say, "Don't ask; pray." Well, I did pray; I was praying now, just as I did at Arzamas. At that time I had prayed simply, like a child. now my prayers had a definite meaning: "If Thou exist, reveal Thy existence to me. To what end am I created? What am I?" I was bowing to the earth, repeating all the prayers I knew, composing new ones; and I was

adding each time, "Reveal Thy existence to me!" I became quiet, waiting for an answer. But no answer came, as if there were nothing to answer. I was alone, alone with myself and was answering my own questions in place of him who would not answer. "What am I created for?" "To live in a future life," I answered. "Then why this uncertainty and torment? I cannot believe in future life. I did believe when I asked, but not with my whole soul. Now I cannot, I cannot! If Thou didst exist, Thou wouldst reveal it to me, to all men. But Thou dost not exist, and there is nothing true but distress." But I cannot accept that! I rebelled against it; I implored Him to reveal His existence to me. I did all that everybody does, but He did not reveal Himself to me. "Ask and it shall be given unto you," I remembered, and began to entreat; in doing so I felt no real comfort, but just surcease of despair. Perhaps it was not entreaty on my part, but only denial of Him. You retreat a step from Him, and He goes from you a mile. I did not believe in Him, and yet here I was entreating Him. But He did not reveal Himself. I was balancing my accounts with Him, and was blaming Him. I simply did not believe.

The next day I used all my endeavors to get through with my affairs somehow during the day, in order to be saved from another night in the hotel room. Although I had not finished everything, I left for home in the evening.

That night at Moscow brought a still greater change into my life, which had been changing ever since the night at Arzamas. I was now paying less attention to my affairs, and grew more and more indifferent to everything around me. my health was also getting bad. My wife urged me to consult a doctor. To her my continual talk about God and religion was a sign of ill-health, whereas I knew I was ill and weak, because of the unsolved questions of religion and of God.

I was trying not to let that question dominate my mind, and continued living amid the old unaltered conditions, filling up my time with incessant occupations. On Sundays and feast days I went to church; I even fasted as I had begun to do since my journey to Pensa, and did not cease to pray. I had no faith in my prayers, but somehow I kept the demand note in my possession instead of tearing it up, and was always presenting it for payment, although I was aware of the impossibility of getting paid. I did it just on the chance. I occupied my days, not with the management of the estate - I felt disgusted with all business because of the struggle it involved - but with the reading of papers, magazines, and novels, and with card-playing for small stakes. the only outlet for my energy was hunting. I had kept that up from habit, having been fond of this sport all my life.

One day in winter, a neighbor of mine came with his dogs to hunt wolves. Having arrived at the meeting place we put on snowshoes to walk over the snow and move rapidly along. The hunt was unsuccessful; the wolves contrived to escape through the stockade. As I became aware of that from a distance, I took the direction of the forest to follow the fresh track of a hare. This led me far away into a field. There I spied the hare, but he had disappeared before I could fire. I turned to go back, and had to pass a forest of huge trees. The snow was deep, the snowshoes were sinking in, and the branches were entangling me. The wood was getting thicker and thicker. I wondered where I was, for the snow had changed all the familiar places. Suddenly I realised that I had lost my way. How should I get home or reach the hunting party? Not a sound to guide me! I was tired and bathed in perspiration. If I stopped, I would probably freeze to death; if I walked on, my strength would forsake me. I shouted, but all was quiet, and no answer came. I turned in the opposite direction, which was wrong again, and looked round. Nothing but the wood on every hand. I could not tell which was east or west. I turned back again, but I could hardly move a step. I was frightened, and stopped. the horror I had experienced in Arzamas and in Moscow seized me again, only a hundred times greater. My heart was beating, my hands and feet were shaking. Am I to die here? I don't want to! Why death? What is death? I was about to ask again, to reproach God, when I suddenly felt I must not; I ought not. I had not the right to present any account to him; He had said all that was necessary, and the fault was wholly mine. I began to implore His forgiveness for I felt disgusted with myself. The horror, however, did not last long. I stood still one moment, plucked up courage, took the direction which seemed to be the right one, and was actually soon out of the wood. I had not been far from its edge when I lost my way. As I came out on the main road, my hands and feet were still shaking, and my heart was beating violently. But my soul was full of joy. I soon found my party, and we all returned home together. I was not quite happy but I knew there was a joy within me which I would understand later on; and that joy proved real. I went to my study to be alone and prayed remembering my sins, and asking for forgiveness. They did not seem to be numerous; but when I thought of what they were they were hateful to me.

Then I began to read the Scriptures. The Old Testament I found incomprehensible but enchanting, the New touching in its meekness. But my favorite reading was now the lives of the saints; they were consoling to me, affording example which seemed more and more possible to follow. Since that time I have grown even less interested in the management of affairs and in family matters. These things even became repulsive to me. Everything was wrong in my eyes. I did not quite realise why they were wrong, but I knew that the things of which my whole life had consisted, now counted for nothing. This was plainly revealed to me again on the occasion of the projected purchase of an estate, which was for sale in our neighborhood on very advantageous terms. I went to inspect it. Everything was very satisfactory, the more so because the peasants on that estate had no land of their own beyond their vegetable gardens. I grasped at once that in exchange for the right of using the landowner's pasture-grounds, they would do all the harvesting for him; and the information I was given proved that I was right. I saw how important that was, and was pleased, as it was in accordance with my old habits of thought. But on my way home I met an old woman who asked her way, and I entered into a conversation with her, during which she told me about her poverty. On returning home, when telling my wife about the advantages the estate afforded, all at once I felt ashamed and disgusted. I said I was not going to buy that estate, for its profits were based on the sufferings of the peasants. I was struck at that moment with the truth of what I was saying, the truth of the peasants having the same desire to live as ourselves, of their being our equals, our brethren, the children of the Father, as the Gospel says. But unexpectedly something which had been gnawing within me for a long time became loosened and was torn away, and something new seemed to be born instead.

My wife was vexed with me and abused me. But I was full of joy. This was the first sign of my madness. My utter madness began to show itself about a month later.

This began by my going to church; I was listening to the Mass with great attention and with a faithful heart, when I was suddenly given a wafer; after which every one began to move forward to kiss the Cross, pushing each other on all sides. As I was leaving church, beggars were standing on the steps. It became instantly clear to me that this ought not to be, and in reality was not. But if this is not, then there is no death and no fear, and nothing is being torn asunder within me, and I am not afraid of any calamity which may come.

At that moment the full light of the truth was kindled in me, and I grew into what I am now. If all this horror does not necessarily exist around me, then it certainly does not exist within me. I distributed on the spot all the money I had among the beggars in the porch, and walked home instead of driving in my carriage as usual, and all the way I talked with the peasants.

Three Deaths

by Leo Tolstoy,

Translated by Nathan Haskell Dole

CHAPTER I

It was autumn.

Along the highway came two equipages at a brisk pace. In the first carriage sat two women. One was a lady, thin and pale; the other, her maid, with a brilliant red complexion, and plump. Her short, dry locks escaped from under a faded cap; her red hand, in a torn glove, put them back with a jerk. Her full bosom, incased in a tapestry shawl, breathed of health; her keen black eyes now gazed through the window at the fields hurrying by them, now rested on her mistress, now peered solicitously into the corners of the coach. Before the maid's face swung the lady's bonnet on the rack; on her knees lay a puppy; her feet were raised by packages lying on the floor, and could almost be heard drumming upon them above the noise of the creaking of the springs and the rattling of the windows. The lady, with her hands resting in her lap and her eyes shut, feebly swayed on the cushions which supported her back, and, slightly frowning, tried to suppress her cough.She wore a white nightcap, and a blue neckerchief twisted around her delicate pale neck. A straight line, disappearing under the cap, parted her perfectly smooth blond hair, which was pomaded; and there was a dry deathly appearance about the whiteness of the skin, in this wide parting. The withered and rather sallow skin was loosely drawn over her delicate and pretty features, and there was a hectic flush on the cheeks and cheekbones. Her lips were dry and restless, her thin eyelashes had lost their curve, and a cloth traveling capote made straight folds over her sunken chest. Although her eyes were closed, her face gave the impression of weariness, irascibility, and habitual suffering. The lackey, leaning back, was napping on the coachbox. The yamshchik, or hired driver, shouting in a clear voice, urged on his four powerful and sweaty horses, occasionally looking back at the other driver, who was shouting just behind them in an open barouche. The tires of the wheels, in their even and rapid course, left wide parallel tracks on the limy mud of the highway.The sky was gray and cold, a moist mist was falling over the fields and the road. It was suffocating in the carriage, and smelt of eau-de-Cologne and dust. The invalid leaned back her head, and slowly opened her eyes. Her great eyes were brilliant, and of a beautiful dark color."Again!" said she, nervously, pushing away with her beautiful attenuated hand the end of her maid's cloak, which occasionally hit against herleg. Her mouth contracted painfully. Matriosha raised her cloak in both hands, lifting herself up on her strong legs, and then sat down again, farther away. Her fresh face was suffused with a brilliant scarlet.The invalid's beautiful dark eyes eagerly followed the maid's motions; and then with both hands she took hold of the seat, and did her best to raise herself a little higher, but her strength was not sufficient.Again her mouth became contracted, and her whole face took on an expression of unavailing, angry irony."If you would only help me ... ah! It's not necessary. I can do it myself. Only have the goodness not to put those pillows behind me. ... On the whole, you had better not touch them, if you don't understand!"The lady closed her eyes, and then again, quickly raising the lids, gazed at her maid. Matriosha looked at her, and gnawed her red lower lip. A heavy sigh escaped from the sick woman's breast; but the sigh was not ended, but was merged in a fit of coughing. She scowled, and turned her face away, clutching her chest with both hands. When the coughing fit was over, she once more shut her eyes, and continued to sit motionless. The coach and the barouche rolled into a village. Matriosha drew her fat hand from under her shawl, and made the sign of the cross."What is this?" demanded the lady."A post-station, madame.""Why did you cross yourself, I should like to know?" "The church, madame."The invalid lady looked out of the window, and began slowly to cross herself, gazing with all her eyes at the great village church, in front of which her carriage was now passing. The two vehicles came to a stop together at the post-house. The sick woman's husband and the doctor dismounted from the barouche, and came to the coach."How are you feeling?" asked the doctor, taking her pulse. "Well, my dear, aren't you fatigued?" asked the husband in French. "Wouldn't you like to get out?" Matriosha, gathering up the bundles, squeezed herself into the corner, so as not to interfere with the conversation."No matter, it's all the same thing," replied the invalid. "I will not get out."The husband, after standing there a little, went into the post-house. Matriosha, jumping from the coach, tiptoed across the muddy road into the enclosure."If I am miserable, there is no reason why the rest of you should not have breakfast," said the sick woman, smiling faintly to the doctor, who was standing by her window. "It makes no difference to them how I am," she remarked to herself as the doctor, turning from her with slow step, started to run up the steps of the station-house. "They are well, and it's all the same to them. O my God!" How now, Eduard Ivanovitch?" said the husband, as he met the doctor, and rubbing his hands with a gay smile. "I have ordered my traveling-case brought; what do you say to that?" "That's worth while," replied the doctor."Well, now, how about her?" asked the husband, with a sigh, lowering his voice and raising his brows. "I have told you that she cannot reach Moscow, much less Italy, especially in such weather." "What is to be done, then? Oh! My God! My God!"The husband covered his eyes with his hand. ... "Give it here," he added, addressing his man, who came bringing the traveling-case."You'll have to stop somewhere on the route," replied the doctor, shrugging his shoulders."But tell me, what can I do?" rejoined the husband. "I have employed every argument to keep her from going; I have spoken to her of our means, and of our children whom we should have to leave behind, and of my business. She would not hear a word. She has made her plans for living abroad, as if she were well. But if I should tell her what her real condition is, it would kill her.""Well, she is a dead woman now; you may as well know it, Vasili Dmitritch. A person cannot live without lungs, and there is no way of making lungs grow again. It is melancholy, it is hard, but what is to be done about it? It is my business and yours to make her last days as easy as possible. The confessor is the person needed here.""Oh, my God! Now just perceive how I am situated, in speaking to her of her last will. Let come whatever may, yet I cannot speak of that. And yet you know how good she is." "Try at least to persuade her to wait until the roads are frozen," said the doctor, shaking his head significantly; "something might happen during the journey." ... "Aksiusha, oh, Aksiusha!" cried the superintendent's daughter, throwing a cloak over her head, and tiptoeing down the muddy back steps. "Come along. Let us have a look at the Shirkinskaya lady; the say she's got lung trouble, and they're taking her abroad. I never saw how any one looked in consumption."Aksiusha jumped down from the door-sill; and the two girls, hand in hand, hurried out of the gates. Shortening their steps, they walked by the coach, and stared in at the lowered window. The invalid bent her head toward them; but, when she saw their inquisitiveness, she frowned and turned away."Oh, de-e-ar!" said the superintendent's daughter, vigorously shaking her head. .... "How wonderfully pretty she used to be, and how she has changed! It is terrible! Did you see? Did you see, Aksiusha?""Yes, andhow thin she is!" assented Aksiusha. "Let us go by and look again; we'll make believe we are going to the well. Did you see, she turned away from us; still I got a good view of her. Isn't it too bad, Masha?""Yes, but what terrible mud!" replied Masha, and both of them started to run back within the gates."It's evident that I have become a fright," thought the sick woman. .... "But we must hurry, hurry, and get abroad, and there I shall soon get well.""Well, and how are you, my dear?" inquired the husband, coming to the coach with still a morsel of something in his mouth. "Always one and the same question," thought the sick woman, "and he's even eating!""It's no consequence," she murmured, between her teeth."Do you know, my dear, I am afraid that this journey in such weather will only make you worse. Edouard Ivanovitch says the same thing. Hadn't we better turn back?" She maintained an angry silence. "Maybe the weather will improve, the roads will become good, and that would be better for you; then at least we could start all together." "Pardon me. If I had not listened to you so long, I should at this moment be at Berlin and have entirely recovered.""What's to be done, my angel? It was impossible, as you know. But now if you would wait a month, you would be ever so much better; I could finish up my business, and we could take the children with us." ...."The children are well, and I am not.""But just see here, my love, if in this weather you should grow worse on the road .... At least we should be at home.""What is the use of being at home? ... Die at home?" replied the invalid, peevishly.But the word die evidently startled her, and she turned on her husband a supplicating and inquiring look. He dropped his eyes, and said nothing.The sick woman's mouth suddenly contracted in a childish fashion, and the tears sprang to her eyes. Her husband covered his face with his handkerchief, and silently turned from the coach."No, I will go," cried the invalid; and, lifting her eyes to the sky, she clasped her hands, and began to whisper incoherent words. "My God! Why must it be?" she said, and the tears flowed more violently.She prayed long and fervently, but still there was just the same sense of constriction and pain in her chest, just the same gray melancholy in the sky and the fields and the road; just the same autumnal mist, neither thicker nor more tenuous, but ever the same it in its monotony, falling on the muddy highway, on the roofs, on the carriage, and on the sheepskin coats of the drivers, who were talking in strong, gay voices, as they were oiling and adjusting the carriage.

CHAPTER II

The coach was ready, but the driver loitered. He had gone into the drivers' room [izba]. In the izba it was warm, close, dark, and suffocating, smelling of human occupation, of cooking bread, of cabbage, and of sheepskin garments.Several drivers were in the room; the cook was engaged near the oven, on top of which lay a sick man wrapped up in his sheepskins."Uncle Khveodor! Hey! Uncle Khveodor," called a young man, the driver, in a tulup, and with his knout in his belt, coming into the room, and addressing the sick man. "What do you want, rattlepate? What are you calling to Fyedka for?" asked one of the drivers. "There's your carriage waiting for you." "I want to borrow his boots. Mine are worn out," replied the young fellow, tossing back his curls and straightening his mittensin his belt. "Why? Is he asleep? Say, Uncle Khvodor!" he insisted, going to the oven."What is it?" a weak voice was heard saying, and an emaciated face was lifted up from the oven. A broad, gaunt hand, bloodless and covered with hairs, pulled up his overcoat over the dirty shirt that covered his bony shoulder. "Give me something to drink, brother; what is it you want?"The young fellow handed him a small dish of water."I say, Fyedya," said he, hesitating, "I reckon you won't want your new boots now; let me have them? Probably you won't need them any more." The sick man, dropping his weary head down to the lacquered bowl, and dipping his thin, hanging mustache into the brown water, drank feebly and eagerly.His tangled beard was unclean; his sunken, clouded eyes were with difficulty raised to the young man's face. When he had finished drinking, he tried to raise his hand to wipe his wet lips, but his strength failed him, and he wiped them on the sleeve of his overcoat. Silently, and breathing with difficulty through his nose, he looked straight into the young man's eyes, and tried to collect his strength. "Maybe you have promised them to some one else?" said the young driver. "If that's so, all right. The worst of it is, it is wet outside, and I have to go out to my work, and so I said to myself, 'I reckon I'll ask Fyedka for his boots; I reckon he won't be needing them.' But may you will need them, -- just say." .... Something began to bubble up and rumble in the sick man's chest; he bent over, and began to strangle, with a cough that rattled in his throat."Now I should like to know where he would need them?" unexpectedly snapped out the cook, angrily addressing the whole hovel. "This is the second month that he has not crept down from the oven. Just see how he is all broken up! And you can hear how it must hurt him inside. Where would he need boots? They would not think of burying him in new ones! And it was time long ago, God pardon me the sin of saying so. Just see how he chokes! He ought to be taken from this room to another, or somewhere. They say there's hospitals in the city; but what's you going to do? He takes up the whole room, and that's too much. There isn't any room at all. And yet you are expected to keep neat." "Hey! Seryoha, come along, take your place, the people are waiting," cried the head man of the station, coming to the door. Seryoha started to go without waiting for his reply, but the sick man during his cough intimated by his eyes that he was going to speak."You take the boots, Seryoha," said he, conquering the cough, and getting his breath a little. "Only, do you hear, buy me a stone when I am dead," he added hoarsely."Thank you, uncle; then I will take them, and as for the stone, -- yei-yei! -- I will buy you one."There, children, you are witnesses," the sick man was able to articulate, and then once more he bent over and began to choke."All right, we have heard," said one of the drivers. "But run, Seryoha, or else the starosta will be after you again. You know Lady Shirkinskaya is sick."Seryoha quickly pulled off his ragged, unwieldy boots, and flung them under the bench. Uncle Feodor's new ones fitted his feet exactly, and the yung driver could not keep his eyes off them as he went to the carriage. "Ek! What splendid boots! Here's some grease," called another driver with the grease-pot in his hand, as Seryoha mounted to his box and gathered up the reins. "Get them for nothing?" "So you're jealous, are you?" cried Seryoha, lifting up and tucking around his legs the tails of his overcoat. "Of with you, my darlings," he cried to the horses, cracking his knout; and the coach and barouche, with their occupants, trunks, and other belongings, were hidden in the thick autumnal mist, and rapidly whirled away over the wet road.The sick driver remained on the oven in the stifling hovel, and, not being able to throw off the phlegm, by a supreme effort turned over on the other side, and stopped coughing. Till evening there was a continual coming and going, and eating of meals in the room, and the sick man was not noticed. Before night came on, the cook climbed up on the oven, and got the ssheepskin coat from the farther side of his legs."Don't be angry with me, Nastasya," exclaimed the sick man. "I shall soon leave your room.""All right, all right, it's of no consequence," muttered the woman. "But what is the matter with you, uncle? Tell me." "All my inwards are gnawed out. God knows what it is!""And I don't doubt your gullet hurts you when you cough so!""It hurts me all over. My death is at hand, that's what it is. Okh! Okh! Okh!" groaned the sick man. "Mow cover up your legs this way," said Nastasya, comfortably arranging the overcoat so that it would cover him, and then getting down from the oven. During the night the room was faintly lighted by a single taper. Nastasya and a dozen drivers were sleeping, snoring loudly, on the floor and the benches. Only the sick man feebly hawked and coughed, and tossed on the oven.In the morning no sound was heard from him."I saw something wonderful in my sleep," said the cook, as she stretched herself in the early twilight the next morning. "I seemed to see Uncle Khveodor get down from the oven and go out to cut wood. 'Look here,' says he, 'I'm going to help you, Nastya;' and I says to him, 'How can you split wood?' but he seizes the hatchet, and begins to cut so fast, so fast that nothing but chips fly. 'Why,' sais I, 'haven't you been sick?' - 'No,' says he, 'I am well,' and he kind of lifted up the ax, and I was scared; and I screamed and woke up. He can't be dead, can he? -- Uncle Khveodor! Hey, uncle!"Feodor did not move."Now he can't be dead, can he? Go and see," said one of the drivers, who had just waked up. The emaciated hand, covered with reddish hair, that hung down from the oven, was cold and pale. "Go tell the superintendent; it seems he is dead," said the driver. Feodor had no relatives. He was a stranger. On the next day they buried him in the new burying-ground behind the grove; and Nastasya for many days had to tell everybody of the vision which she had seen, and how she had been the first to discover that Uncle Feodor was dead.

CHAPTER III

Spring had come. Along the wet streets of the city swift streamlets ran purling between heaps of dung-covered ice; bright were the colors of people's dresses and the tones of their voices, as they hurried along. In the walled gardens, the buds on the trees were burgeoning, and the fresh breeze swayed their branches with a soft gentle murmur. Everywhere transparent drops were forming and falling. .... The sparrows chattered incoherently, and fluttered about on their little wings. On the sunny side, on the walls, houses, and trees, all was full of life and brilliancy. The sky, and the earth, and the heart of man overflowed with youth and joy. In front of a great seigniorial mansion, in one of the principal streets, fresh straw had been laid down; in the house lay that same moribund invalid whom we saw hastening abroad. Near the closed doors of her room stood the sick lady's husband, and a lady well along in years. On a divan sat the confessor, with cast-down eyes, holding something wrapped up under his stole. In one corner, in a Voltaire easy-chair, reclined an old lady, the sick woman's mother, weeping violently. Near her stood the maid, holding a clean handkerchief, ready for the old lady's use when she should ask for it. Another maid was rubbing the old lady's temples, and blowing on her gray head underneath her cap. "Well, Christ be with you, my dear," said the husband to the elderly lady who was standing with him near the door: "she has such confidence in you; you know how to talk with her; go and speak with her a little while, my darling, please go!" He was about to open the door for her; but his cousin held him back, putting her handkerchief several times to her eyes, and shaking her head. "There, now she will not see that I have been weeping," said she, and, opening the door herself, went to the invalid. The husband was in the greatest excitement, and seemed quite beside himself. He started to go over to the old mother, but, after taking a few steps, he turned around, walked the length of the room, and approached the priest.The priest looked at him, raised his brows toward heaven, and sighed. The thick gray beard also was lifted and fell again."My God! My God!" said the husband."What can you do?" exclaimed the confessor, sighing and again lifting up his brows and beard, and letting them drop."And the old mother there!" exclaimed the husband almost in despair. "She will not be able to endure it. You see, she loved her so, she loved her so, that she .... I don't know. You might try, father, to calm her a little, and persuade her to go away."The confessor arose and went over to the old lady."It is true, no one can appreciate a mother's heart," said he, "but God is compassionate."

The old lady's face was suddenly convulsed, and a hysterical sob shook her frame."God is compassionate," repeated the priest, when she had grown a little calmer. "I will tell you, in my parish there was a sick man, and much worse than Marya Dmitrievna, and he, though he was only a shopkeeper, was cured in a very short time, by means of herbs. And this very same shopkeeper is now in Moscow. I have told Vasili Dmitrievitch about him; it might be tried, you know. At all events, it would satisfy the invalid. With God, all things are possible.""No, she won't get well," persisted the old lady. "Why should God have taken her, and not me?"And again the hysterical sobbing overcame her, so violently that she fainted away. The invalid's husband hid his face in his hands, and rushed from the room.In the corridor the first person whom he met was a six-year-old boy, who was chasing his little sister with all his might and main."Do you bid me take the children to their mamasha?" inquired the nurse."No, she does not like to see them. They distract her."The lad stopped for a moment, and, after looking eagerly into his father's face, he cut a dido with his leg, and with merry shouts ran on."I'm playing whe's a horse, papasha," cried the little fellow, pointing to his sister. Meantime, in the next room, the cousin had taken her seat near the sick woman, and was skilfully bringing the conversation by degrees round so as to prepare her for the thought of death. The doctor stood by the window, mixing some draught.The invalid, in a white capote, all surrounded by cushions, was sitting up in bed, and gazed silently at her cousin."Ah, my dear!" she exclaimed, unexpectedly interrupting her, "don't try to prepare me; don't treat me like a little child! I am a Christian woman. I know all about it. I know that I have not long to live; I know that if my husband had heeded me sooner, I should have been in Italy, and possibly, yes probably, should have been well by this time. They all told him so. But what is to be done? It's as God saw fit. We all of us have sinned, I know that; but I hope in the mercy of God, that all will be pardoned, ought to be pardoned. I am trying to sound my own heart. I also have committed many sins, my love. But how much I have suffered in atonement! I have tried to bear my sufferings patiently." .... "Then shall I have the confessor come in, my love? It will be all the easier for you, after you have been absolved," said the cousin.The sick woman dropped her head in token of assent. "O God! Pardon me, a sinner," she whispered.The cousin went out, and beckoned to the confessor. "She is an angel," she said to the husband, with tears in her eyes. The husband wept. The priest went into the sick room; the old lady still remained unconscious, and in the room beyond all was perfectly quiet. At the end of five minutes the confessor came out, and, taking off his stole, arranged his hair."Thanks be to the Lord, she is calmer now," said he. "She wishes to see you."The cousin and the husband went to the sick room. The invalid, gently weeping, was gazing at the images. "I congratulate you, my love," said the husband."Thank you. How well I feel now! What ineffable joy I experience!" said the sick woman, and a faint smile played over her thin lips. "How merciful God is! Is He not? He is merciful and omnipotent!"And again with an eager prayer she turned her tearful eyes toward the holy images.Then suddenly something seemed to occur to her mind. She beckoned to her husband."You are never willing to do what I desire," said she, in a weak and querulous voice.The husband, stretching his neck, listened to her submissively."What is it, my love?""How many times I have told you that these doctors don't know anything! There are simple women doctors; they make cures. That's what the good father said. ... A shopkeeper .... Send for him." ..."For whom, my love?" "Good heavens! You can never understand me." And the dying woman frowned, and closed her eyes. The doctor came to her, and took her hand. Her pulse was evidently growing feebler and feebler. He made a sign to the husband. The sick woman remarked this gesture, and looked around in fright. The cousin turned away to hide her tears. "Don't weep, don't torment yourselves on my account," said the invalid. "That takes away from me my last comfort.""You are an angel!" exclaimed the cousin, kissing her hand."No, kiss me here. They only kiss the hands of those who are dead. My God! My God!" That same evening the sick woman was a corpse, and the corpse in the coffin lay in the parlor of the great mansion. In the immense room, the doors of which were closed, sat the clerk, and with a monstrous voice read the Psalms of David through his nose. The bright glare from the wax candles in the lofty silver candelabra fell on the white brow of the dead, on the heavy waxen hands, on the stiff folds of the cerement which brought out into awful relief the knees and the feet.The clerk, not varying his tones, continued to read on steadily, and in the silence of the chamber of death his words rang out and died away. Occasionally from distant rooms came the voice of children and their romping. "Thou hidest thy face, they are troubled; thou takest away their breath, they die and return to their dust."Thou sendest forth thy Spirit, they are created; and thou renewest the fact of the earth. "The glor of the Lord shall endure forever." ... The face of the dead was stern and majestic. But there was no motion either on the pure cold brow, or the firmly closed lips. She was all attention! But did she perhaps now understand these majestic words?

CHAPTER IV

At the end of a month, over the grave of the dead a stone chapel was erected. Over the driver's there was as yet no stone, and only the fresh green grass sprouted over the mound which served as the sole record of the past existence of a man.

"It will be a sin and a shame, Seryoha," said the cook at the station-house one day, "if you don't buy a gravestone for Khveodor. You kept saying, 'it's winter, winter,' but now why don't you keep your word? I heard it all. He has already come back once to ask why you don't do it; if you don't buy him one, he will come again, he will choke you." "Well, now, have I denied it?" urged Seryoha. "I am going to buy him a stone, as I said I would. I can get one for a ruble and a half. I have not forgotten about it; I'll have to get it. As soon as I happen to be in town, then I'll buy him one.""You ought at least to put up a cross, that's what you ought to do," said an old driver. It isn't right at all. You're wearing those boots now." "Yes. But where could I get him a cross? You wouldn't want to make one out of an old piece of stick, would you?""What is that you say? Make one out of an old piece of stick? No; take your ax, go out to the wood a little earlier than usual, and you can hew him out one. Take a little ash tree, and you can make one. You can have a covered cross. If you go then, you won't have to give the watchman a little drink of vodka. One doesn't want to give vodka for every trifle. Now, yesterday I broke my axletree, and I go and hew out a new one of green wood.

No one said a word." Early the next morning, almost before dawn, Seryoha took his ax, and went to the wood.Over all things hung a cold, dead veil of falling mist, as yet untouched by the rays of the sun.The east gradually grew brighter, reflecting its pale light over the vault of heaven still covered by light clouds. Not a single grass-blade below, now a single leaf on the topmost branches of the tree-top, waved. Only from time to time could be heard the sound of fluttering wings in the thicket, or a rustling on the ground broke in on the silence of the forest. Suddenly a strange sound, foreign to this nature, resounded and died away at the edge of the forest. Again the noise sounded, and was monotonously repeated again and again, at the foot of one of the ancient, immovable trees. A tree-top began to shake in an extraordinary manner; the juicy leaves whispered something; and the warbler, sitting on one of the branches, flew off a couple of times with a shrill cry, and wagging its tail, finally perched on another tree. The ax rang more and more frequently; the white chips, full of sap, were scattered upon the dewy grass, and a slight cracking was heard beneath the blows. The tree trembled with all its body, leaned over, and quickly straightened itself, shuddering with fear on its base. For an instant all was still, then once more the tree bent over; a crash was heard in its trunk; and, tearing the thicket, and dragging down the branches, it plunged toward the damp earth. The noise of the ax and of footsteps ceased. The warbler uttered a cry, and flew higher. The branch which she grazed with her wings shook for an instant, and then came to rest like all the others their foliage. The trees, more joyously than ever, extended their motionless branches over the new space that had been made in their midst. The first sunbeams, breaking through the cloud, gleamed in the sky, and shone along the earth and heavens. The mist, in billows, began to float along the hollows; the dew, gleaming, played on the green foliage; translucent white clouds hurried along their azure path. The birds hopped about in the thicket, and, as if beside themselves, voiced their happiness; the juicy leaves joyfully and contentedly whispered on the tree-tops; and the branches of the living trees slowly and majestically waved over the dead and fallen tree.

Leo Tolstoy

Born
Lev Nikolayevich Tolstoy
September 9, 1828
Yasnaya Polyana, Russian Empire

Count Lev Nikolayevich Tolstoy; 9 September [O.S. 28 August] 1828 – 20 November [O.S. 7 November] 1910), usually referred to in English as Leo Tolstoy, was a Russian novelist. He is regarded as one of the greatest in the canon of world literature.

His best known works are War and Peace (1869) and Anna Karenina (1877). He first achieved literary acclaim in his 20s with the semi-autobiographical trilogy, Childhood, Boyhood, and Youth (1852–1856), and Sevastopol Sketches (1855), the latter based upon his experiences in the Crimean War. Tolstoy's fiction includes dozens of short stories and several novellas such as The Death of Ivan Ilyich, Family Happiness, and Hadji Murad. He also wrote plays and numerous philosophical essays.

In the 1870s Tolstoy experienced a moral crisis, followed by what he regarded as a profound spiritual awakening, as outlined in his non-fiction work A Confession. His literal interpretation of the ethical teachings of Jesus, centering on the Sermon on the Mount, caused him to become a fervent Christian anarchist and pacifist. His new-found asceticism and determination to renounce his considerable wealth tipped his marriage into turmoil, which continued right up to his death at the age of 82, in the waiting room of an, until then, obscure Russian railway station.

Tolstoy's ideas on nonviolent resistance, expressed in such works as The Kingdom of God Is Within You, were to have a significant impact on such pivotal 20th-century figures as Mohandas Gandhi,[2] Martin Luther King, Jr.,[3] and James Bevel.

Life and career

Tolstoy was born at Yasnaya Polyana, a family estate located 12 kilometres (7.5 mi) southwest of Tula, Russia and 200 kilometers (120 mi) south of Moscow. The Tolstoys were a well-known family of old Russian nobility, tracing their ancestry to a mythical Lithuanian noble Indris.[4][5] He was the fourth of five children of Count Nikolai Ilyich Tolstoy, a veteran of the Patriotic War of 1812, and Countess Mariya Tolstaya (Volkonskaya). Tolstoy's parents died when he was young, so he and his siblings were brought up by relatives. In 1844, he began studying law and oriental languages at Kazan University. His teachers described him as "both unable and unwilling to learn."[6] Tolstoy left the university in the middle of his studies, returned to Yasnaya Polyana and then spent much of his time in Moscow and Saint Petersburg. In 1851, after running up heavy gambling debts, he went with his older brother to the Caucasus and joined the army. It was about this time that he started writing.

His conversion from a dissolute and privileged society author to the non-violent and spiritual anarchist of his latter days was brought about by his experience in the army as well as two trips around Europe in 1857 and 1860–61. Others who followed the same path were Alexander Herzen, Mikhail Bakunin and Peter Kropotkin. During his 1857 visit, Tolstoy witnessed a public execution in Paris, a traumatic experience that would mark the rest of his life. Writing in a letter to his friend Vasily Botkin: "The truth is that the State is a conspiracy designed not only to exploit, but above all to corrupt its citizens ... Henceforth, I shall never serve any government anywhere."[7]

His European trip in 1860–61 shaped both his political and literary development when he met Victor Hugo, whose literary talents Tolstoy praised after reading Hugo's newly finished Les Misérables. The similar evocation of battle scenes in Hugo's novel and Tolstoy's War and Peace indicates this influence. Tolstoy's political philosophy was also influenced by a March 1861 visit to French anarchist Pierre-Joseph Proudhon, then living in exile under an assumed name in Brussels. Apart from reviewing Proudhon's forthcoming publication, La Guerre et la Paix (War and Peace in French), whose title Tolstoy would borrow for his masterpiece, the two men discussed education, as Tolstoy wrote in his educational notebooks: "If I recount this conversation with Proudhon, it is to show that, in my personal experience, he was the only man who understood the significance of education and of the printing press in our time."

Fired by enthusiasm, Tolstoy returned to Yasnaya Polyana and founded 13 schools for children of Russia's peasants, who had just been emancipated from serfdom in 1861. Tolstoy described the school's principles in his 1862 essay "The School at Yasnaya Polyana".[8] Tolstoy's educational experiments were short-lived, partly due to harassment by the Tsarist secret police. However, as a direct forerunner to A. S. Neill's Summerhill School, the school at Yasnaya Polyana[9] can justifiably be claimed the first example of a coherent theory of democratic education.

Death

Tolstoy died in 1910, at the age of 82. Prior to this, his health had been a concern of his family, who were actively engaged in his care on a daily basis. During his last few days, he had spoken and written about dying. Renouncing his aristocratic lifestyle, he had separated from his wife and left home during the night and in the middle of winter.[10] His secretive departure was an apparent attempt to escape unannounced from his wife's attention. She was outspokenly opposed to many of his teachings, and in recent years had grown envious of the attention which, it seemed to her, Tolstoy gave to his Tolstoyan followers.

Tolstoy died of pneumonia[11] at Astapovo train station, after a day's rail journey south.[12] The station master took Tolstoy to his apartment, and his personal doctors were called to the scene. He was given injections of morphine and camphor. The police tried to limit access to his funeral procession, but thousands of peasants lined the streets, though many knew little about Tolstoy.[13] According to some sources, Tolstoy spent the last hours of his life preaching love, nonviolence, and Georgism to his fellow passengers on the train.[14]

Personal life

On September 23, 1862, Tolstoy married Sophia Andreevna Behrs, who was 16 years his junior and the daughter of a court physician. She was called Sonya, the Russian diminutive of Sofia, by her family and friends.[15] They had 13 children, eight of whom survived childhood:[16]

Countess Tatyana Lvovna Tolstaya (October 4, 1864 – September 21, 1950), wife of Mikhail Sergeevich Sukhotin
Count Ilya Lvovich Tolstoy (May 22, 1866 – December 11, 1933), writer
Count Lev Lvovich Tolstoy (June 1, 1869 – October 18, 1945), writer and sculptor
Countess Maria Lvovna Tolstaya (1871–1906), wife of Nikolai Leonidovich Obolensky
Count Peter Lvovich Tolstoy (1872–1873), died in infancy

Count Nikolai Lvovich Tolstoy (1874–1875), died in infancy
Countess Varvara Lvovna Tolstaya (1875–1875), died in infancy
Count Andrei Lvovich Tolstoy (1877–1916), served in the Russo-Japanese War
Count Michael Lvovich Tolstoy (1879–1944)
Count Alexei Lvovich Tolstoy (1881–1886)
Countess Alexandra Lvovna Tolstaya (July 18, 1884 – September 26, 1979)
Count Ivan Lvovich Tolstoy (1888–1895)

The marriage was marked from the outset by sexual passion and emotional insensitivity when Tolstoy, on the eve of their marriage, gave her his diaries detailing his extensive sexual past and the fact that one of the serfs on his estate had borne him a son.[15] Even so, their early married life was ostensibly happy and allowed Tolstoy much freedom to compose War and Peace and Anna Karenina with Sonya acting as his secretary, proofreader and financial manager.[15]

However, their later life together has been described by A. N. Wilson as one of the unhappiest in literary history. Tolstoy's relationship with his wife deteriorated as his beliefs became increasingly radical. This saw him seeking to reject his inherited and earned wealth, including the renunciation of the copyrights on his earlier works.

The Tolstoy family left Russia in the aftermath of the Russian Revolution, and Leo Tolstoy's descendants today live in Sweden, Germany, the United Kingdom, France and the United States. Among them are Swedish singer Viktoria Tolstoy and Swedish landowner Christopher Paus, Herresta.

Novels and fictional works

Tolstoy is one of the most significant figures in Russian literature; his works include the novels War and Peace and Anna Karenina and novellas such as Hadji Murad and The Death of Ivan Ilyich. His contemporary Fyodor Dostoyevsky thought him the best of all then living novelists; Gustave Flaubert praised the artistry and psychology of War and Peace. Anton Chekhov, who often visited Tolstoy at his country estate, wrote, "When literature possesses a Tolstoy, it is easy and pleasant to be a writer; even when you know you have achieved nothing yourself and are still achieving nothing, this is not as terrible as it might otherwise be, because Tolstoy achieves for everyone. What he does serves to justify all the hopes and aspirations invested in literature."

Later critics and novelists continued to praise Tolstoy's art. Virginia Woolf declared him the greatest of all novelists. James Joyce noted that, "He is never dull, never stupid, never tired, never pedantic, never theatrical!". Thomas Mann wrote of Tolstoy's seemingly guileless artistry: "Seldom did art work so much like nature". Such sentiments were shared by Proust, Faulkner and Nabokov.

Tolstoy's earliest works, the autobiographical novels Childhood, Boyhood, and Youth (1852–1856), tell of a rich landowner's son and his slow realization of the chasm between himself and his peasants. Though he later rejected them as sentimental, they deal with Tolstoy's own life.

Tolstoy served as a second lieutenant in an artillery regiment during the Crimean War, recounted in his Sevastopol Sketches. His experiences in battle influenced his subsequent pacifism and gave him material for the realistic depiction of war in his later work.[17]

His fiction consistently attempts to convey realistically the Russian society in which he lived.[18] The Cossacks (1863) describes the Cossack life and people through a story of a Russian aristocrat in love with a Cossack girl. Anna Karenina (1877) tells parallel stories of an adulterous woman trapped by the conventions and falsities of society and of a philosophical landowner (much like Tolstoy), who works alongside the peasants in the fields and seeks to reform their lives. Tolstoy not only drew from his own life experiences but also created characters in his own image, such as Pierre Bezukhov and Prince Andrei in War and Peace, Levin in Anna Karenina and to some extent, Prince Nekhlyudov in Resurrection.

The Power of Darkness

War and Peace is generally thought to be one history's greatest novels, remarkable for its dramatic breadth and unity. Its canvas includes 580 characters, many historical while others are fictional. The story moves from family life to the headquarters of Napoleon, from the court of Alexander I of Russia to the battlefields of Austerlitz and Borodino. Tolstoy's original idea for the novel was to investigate the causes of the Decembrist revolt, to which it refers only in the last chapters, from which can be deduced that Andrei Bolkonsky's son will become one of the Decembrists. The novel explores Tolstoy's theory of history, and in particular the insignificance of individuals such as Napoleon and Alexander. Tolstoy did not consider War and Peace to be a novel (nor did he consider many of the great Russian fictions written at that time to be novels): Tolstoy was a novelist of the realist school who considered the novel to be a framework for the examination of social and political issues in nineteenth-century life.[19] War and Peace (which is to Tolstoy really an epic in prose) therefore did not qualify. Tolstoy thought that Anna Karenina was his first true novel.[20]

After Anna Karenina, Tolstoy concentrated on Christian themes, and his later novels such as The Death of Ivan Ilyich (1886) and What Is to Be Done? develop a radical anarcho-pacifist Christian philosophy which led to his excommunication from the Russian Orthodox Church in 1901.[21] Despite the acclaim for Anna Karenina and War and Peace, Tolstoy rejected the two works later in his life as something not as true of reality.[22] In his novel Resurrection, Tolstoy attempts to expose the injustice of man-made laws and the hypocrisy of the institutionalized church. Tolstoy also explores and explains the economic philosophy of Georgism, of which he had become a very strong advocate towards the end of his life.

Religious and political beliefs

After reading Schopenhauer's The World as Will and Representation, Tolstoy gradually became converted to the ascetic morality upheld in that work as the proper spiritual path for the upper classes: "Do you know what this summer has meant for me? Constant raptures over Schopenhauer and a whole series of spiritual delights which I've never experienced before. ... no student has ever studied so much on his course, and learned so much, as I have this summer"[23]

In Chapter VI of A Confession, Tolstoy quoted the final paragraph of Schopenhauer's work. It explained how the nothingness that results from complete denial of self is only a relative nothingness, and is not to be feared. The novelist was struck by the description of Christian, Buddhist, and Hindu ascetic renunciation as being the path to holiness. After reading passages such as the following, which abound in Schopenhauer's ethical chapters, the Russian nobleman chose poverty and formal denial of the will:

But this very necessity of involuntary suffering (by poor people) for eternal salvation is also expressed by that utterance of the Savior (Matthew 19:24): "It is easier for a camel to go through the eye of a needle, than for a rich man to enter into the kingdom of God." Therefore those who were greatly in earnest about their eternal salvation, chose voluntary poverty when fate had denied this to them and they had been born in wealth. Thus Buddha Sakyamuni was born a prince, but voluntarily took to the mendicant's staff; and Francis of Assisi, the founder of the mendicant orders who, as a youngster at a ball, where the daughters of all the notabilities were sitting together, was asked: "Now Francis, will you not soon make your choice from these beauties?" and who replied: "I have made a far more beautiful choice!" "Whom?" "La povertà (poverty)": whereupon he abandoned every thing shortly afterwards and wandered through the land as a mendicant.[24]

In 1884, Tolstoy wrote a book called "What I Believe", in which he openly confessed his Christian beliefs. He affirmed his belief in Jesus Christ's teachings and was particularly influenced by the Sermon on the Mount, and the injunction to turn the other cheek, which he understood as a "commandment of non-resistance to evil by force" and a doctrine of pacifism and nonviolence. In his work The Kingdom of God Is Within You, he explains that he considered mistaken the Church's doctrine because they had made a "perversion" of Christ's teachings. Tolstoy also received letters from American Quakers who introduced him to the non-violence writings of Quaker Christians such as George Fox, William Penn and Jonathan Dymond. Tolstoy believed being a Christian required him to be a pacifist; the consequences of being a pacifist, and the apparently inevitable waging of war by government, are the reason why he is considered a philosophical anarchist.

Later, various versions of "Tolstoy's Bible" would be published, indicating the passages Tolstoy most relied on, specifically, the reported words of Jesus himself.[25]

Tolstoy believed that a true Christian could find lasting happiness by striving for inner self-perfection through following the Great Commandment of loving one's neighbor and God rather than looking outward to the Church or state for guidance. His belief in nonresistance when faced by conflict is another distinct attribute of his philosophy based on Christ's teachings. By directly influencing Mahatma Gandhi with this idea through his work The Kingdom of God Is Within You (full text of English translation available on Wikisource), Tolstoy's profound influence on the nonviolent resistance movement reverberates to this day. He believed that the aristocracy were a burden on the poor, and that the only solution to how we live together is through anarchism.[citation needed]

He also opposed private property in land ownership[26] and the institution of marriage and valued the ideals of chastity and sexual abstinence (discussed in Father Sergius and his preface to The Kreutzer Sonata), ideals also held by the young Gandhi. Tolstoy's later work derives a passion and verve from the depth of his austere moral views.[27] The sequence of the temptation of Sergius in Father Sergius, for example, is among his later triumphs. Gorky relates how Tolstoy once read this passage before himself and Chekhov and that Tolstoy was moved to tears by the end of the reading. Other later passages of rare power include the personal crises that were faced by the protagonists of The Death of Ivan Ilyich, and of Master and Man, where the main character in the former or the reader in the latter are made aware of the foolishness of the protagonists' lives.

Tolstoy had a profound influence on the development of Christian anarchist thought.[28] The Tolstoyans were a small Christian anarchist group formed by Tolstoy's companion, Vladimir Chertkov (1854–1936), to spread Tolstoy's religious teachings. Philosopher Peter Kropotkin wrote of Tolstoy in the article on anarchism in the 1911 Encyclopædia Britannica:

Without naming himself an anarchist, Leo Tolstoy, like his predecessors in the popular religious movements of the 15th and

16th centuries, Chojecki, Denk and many others, took the anarchist position as regards the state and property rights, deducing his conclusions from the general spirit of the teachings of Jesus and from the necessary dictates of reason. With all the might of his talent, Tolstoy made (especially in The Kingdom of God Is Within You) a powerful criticism of the church, the state and law altogether, and especially of the present property laws. He describes the state as the domination of the wicked ones, supported by brutal force. Robbers, he says, are far less dangerous than a well-organized government. He makes a searching criticism of the prejudices which are current now concerning the benefits conferred upon men by the church, the state, and the existing distribution of property, and from the teachings of Jesus he deduces the rule of non-resistance and the absolute condemnation of all wars. His religious arguments are, however, so well combined with arguments borrowed from a dispassionate observation of the present evils, that the anarchist portions of his works appeal to the religious and the non-religious reader alike.[29]

During the Boxer Rebellion in China, Tolstoy praised the Boxers. He was harshly critical of the atrocities committed by the Russians, Germans, and other western troops. He accused them of engaging in slaughter when he heard about the lootings, rapes, and murders, in what he saw as Christian brutality. Tolstoy also named the two monarchs most responsible for the atrocities; Nicholas II of Russia and Wilhelm II of Germany.[30][31] Tolstoy, a famous sinophile, also read the works of Chinese thinker and philosopher, Confucius.[32][33][34] Tolstoy corresponded with the Chinese intellectual Gu Hongming and recommended that China remain an agrarian nation and warned against reform like what Japan implemented.

In hundreds of essays over the last 20 years of his life, Tolstoy reiterated the anarchist critique of the state and recommended books by Kropotkin and Proudhon to his readers, whilst rejecting anarchism's espousal of violent revolutionary means. In the 1900 essay, "On Anarchy", he wrote; "The Anarchists are right in everything; in the negation of the existing order, and in the assertion that, without Authority, there could not be worse violence than that of Authority under existing conditions. They are mistaken only in thinking that Anarchy can be instituted by a revolution. But it will be instituted only by there being more and more people who do not require the protection of governmental power ... There can be only one permanent revolution—a moral one: the regeneration of the inner man." Despite his misgivings about anarchist violence, Tolstoy took risks to circulate the prohibited publications of anarchist thinkers in Russia, and corrected the proofs of Kropotkin's "Words of a Rebel", illegally published in St Petersburg in 1906.[35]

Tolstoy was enthused by the economic thinking of Henry George, incorporating it approvingly into later works such as Resurrection (1899), the book that played a major factor in his excommunication.[36]

In 1908, Tolstoy wrote A Letter to a Hindu[37] outlining his belief in non-violence as a means for India to gain independence from British colonial rule. In 1909, a copy of the letter was read by Mohandas Gandhi, who was working as a lawyer in South Africa at the time and just becoming an activist. Tolstoy's letter was significant for Gandhi, who wrote Tolstoy seeking proof that he was the real author, leading to further correspondence between them.[38]

Reading Tolstoy's The Kingdom of God Is Within You also convinced Gandhi to avoid violence and espouse nonviolent resistance, a debt Gandhi acknowledged in his autobiography, calling Tolstoy "the greatest apostle of non-violence that the present age has produced". The correspondence between Tolstoy and Gandhi would only last a year, from October 1909 until Tolstoy's death in

November 1910, but led Gandhi to give the name Tolstoy Colony to his second ashram in South Africa.[39] Besides nonviolent resistance, the two men shared a common belief in the merits of vegetarianism, the subject of several of Tolstoy's essays.[40]

Tolstoy also became a major supporter of the Esperanto movement. Tolstoy was impressed by the pacifist beliefs of the Doukhobors and brought their persecution to the attention of the international community, after they burned their weapons in peaceful protest in 1895. He aided the Doukhobors in migrating to Canada.[41] In 1904, during the Russo-Japanese War, Tolstoy condemned the war and wrote to the Japanese Buddhist priest Soyen Shaku in a failed attempt to make a joint pacifist statement.

Towards the end of his life, Tolstoy become more and more occupied with the economic theory and social philosophy of Georgism.[42][43][44][45] He spoke of great admiration of Henry George, stating once that "People do not argue with the teaching of George; they simply do not know it. And it is impossible to do otherwise with his teaching, for he who becomes acquainted with it cannot but agree."[46] He also wrote a preface to George's Social Problems.[47] Tolstoy and George both rejected private property in land (the most important source of income of the passive Russian aristocracy that Tolstoy so heavily criticized) whilst simultaneously both rejecting a centrally planned socialist economy. Some assume that this development in Tolstoy's thinking was a move away from his anarchist views, since Georgism requires a central administration to collect land rent and spend it on infrastructure. However, anarchist versions of Georgism have also been proposed since.[48] Tolstoy's 1899 novel Resurrection explores his thoughts on Georgism in more detail and hints that Tolstoy indeed had such a view. It suggests the possibility of small communities with some form of local governance to manage the collective land rents for common goods; whilst still heavily criticising institutions of the state such as the justice system.

In films

A 2009 film about Tolstoy's final year, The Last Station, based on the novel by Jay Parini, was made by director Michael Hoffman with Christopher Plummer as Tolstoy and Helen Mirren as Sofya Tolstoya. Both performers were nominated for Oscars for their roles. There have been other films about the writer, including Departure of a Grand Old Man, made in 1912 just two years after his death, How Fine, How Fresh the Roses Were (1913), and Leo Tolstoy, directed by and starring Sergei Gerasimov in 1984.

There is also a famous lost film of Tolstoy made a decade before he died. In 1901, the American travel lecturer Burton Holmes visited Yasnaya Polyana with Albert J. Beveridge, the U.S. senator and historian. As the three men conversed, Holmes filmed Tolstoy with his 60-mm movie camera. Afterwards, Beveridge's advisers succeeded in having the film destroyed, fearing that documentary evidence of a meeting with the Russian author might hurt Beveridge's chances of running for the U.S. presidency.[49]